# SAUDI ARABIA AND THE NEW STRATEGIC LANDSCAPE

HERBERT AND JANE DWIGHT WORKING GROUP
ON ISLAMISM AND THE INTERNATIONAL ORDER

*Many of the writings associated with this
Working Group will be published by the
Hoover Institution. Materials published to date,
or in production, are listed below.*

ESSAYS

*Saudi Arabia and the New Strategic Landscape*
Joshua Teitelbaum

*Islamism and the Future of the Christians of the Middle East*
Habib C. Malik

*Syria through Jihadist Eyes: A Perfect Enemy*
Nibras Kazimi

*The Ideological Struggle for Pakistan*
Ziad Haider

BOOKS

*Freedom or Terror: Europe Faces Jihad*
Russell A. Berman

# SAUDI ARABIA AND THE NEW STRATEGIC LANDSCAPE

Joshua Teitelbaum

HOOVER INSTITUTION PRESS
Stanford University          Stanford, California

www.hoover.org

Hoover Institution Press Publication No. 586
Hoover Institution at Leland Stanford Junior University,
Stanford, California, 94305–6010

First printing 2010
16  15  14  13  12  11  10      9 8 7 6 5 4 3 2 1

Manufactured in the United States of America

The paper used in this publication meets the minimum Requirements of the American National Standard for Information Sciences— Permanence of Paper for Printed Library Materials, ANSI/NISO Z39.48–1992. ⊗

Cataloging-in-Publication Data is available from the Library of Congress.
ISBN 978-0-8179-1105-8 (pbk)
ISBN 978-0-8179-1106-5 (e-book)

*The Hoover Institution gratefully acknowledges*
*the following individuals and foundations*
*for their significant support of the*

# HERBERT AND JANE DWIGHT WORKING GROUP
# ON ISLAMISM AND THE INTERNATIONAL ORDER

**Herbert and Jane Dwight**
**Stephen Bechtel Foundation**
**Lynde and Harry Bradley Foundation**
**Mr. and Mrs. Clayton W. Frye Jr.**
**Lakeside Foundation**

# CONTENTS

# FOREWORD

FOR DECADES, the themes of the Hoover Institution have revolved around the broad concerns of political and economic and individual freedom. The cold war that engaged and challenged our nation during the twentieth century guided a good deal of Hoover's work, including its archival accumulation and research studies. The steady output of work on the communist world offers durable testimonies to that time, and struggle. But there is no repose from history's exertions, and no sooner had communism left the stage of history than a huge challenge arose in the broad lands of the Islamic world. A brief respite, and a meandering road, led from the fall of the Berlin Wall on 11/9 in 1989 to 9/11. Hoover's newly launched project, the Herbert and Jane Dwight Working

Group on Islamism and the International Order, is our contribution to a deeper understanding of the struggle in the Islamic world between order and its nemesis, between Muslims keen to protect the rule of reason and the gains of modernity, and those determined to deny the Islamic world its place in the modern international order of states. The United States is deeply engaged, and dangerously exposed, in the Islamic world, and we see our working group as part and parcel of the ongoing confrontation with the radical Islamists who have declared war on the states in their midst, on American power and interests, and on the very order of the international state system.

The Islamists are doubtless a minority in the world of Islam. But they are a determined breed. Their world is the Islamic emirate, led by self-styled "emirs and mujahedeen in the path of God" and legitimized by the pursuit of the caliphate that collapsed with the end of the Ottoman Empire in 1924. These masters of terror and their foot soldiers have made it increasingly difficult to integrate the world of Islam into modernity. In the best of worlds, the entry of Muslims into modern culture and economics would have presented difficulties of no small consequence: the strictures on women, the legacy of humiliation and self-pity, the outdated educational systems, and an explosive demography that is forever at war with social and economic gains. But the borders these warriors of the faith have erected between Islam and "the other" are particularly forbidding. The lands of Islam were the lands of a crossroads civilization, trading routes and mixed populations. The Islamists have waged war, and a brutally effective one it has to be conceded, against that civilizational inheritance. The leap into the modern world economy as attained by China and India in recent years will be virtually impossible in a culture that feeds off belligerent self-pity, and endlessly calls for wars of faith.

The war of ideas with radical Islamism is inescapably central to this Hoover endeavor. The strategic context of this clash, the landscape of that Greater Middle East, is the other pillar. We face three layers of danger in the heartland of the Islamic world: states that have succumbed to the sway of terrorists in which state authority no longer exists (Afghanistan, Somalia, and Yemen), dictatorial regimes that suppress their people at home and pursue deadly weapons of mass destruction and adventurism abroad (Iraq under Saddam Hussein, the Iranian theocracy), and "enabler" regimes, such as the ones in Egypt and Saudi Arabia, which export their own problems with radical Islamism to other parts of the Islamic world and beyond. In this context, the task of reversing Islamist radicalism and of reforming and strengthening the state across the entire Muslim world—the Middle East, Africa, as well as South, Southeast, and Central Asia—is the greatest strategic challenge of the twenty-first century. The essential starting point is detailed knowledge of our enemy.

Thus, the working group will draw on the intellectual resources of Hoover and Stanford and on an array of scholars and practitioners from elsewhere in the United States, from the Middle East, and the broader world of Islam. The scholarship on contemporary Islam can now be read with discernment. A good deal of it, produced in the immediate aftermath of 9/11, was not particularly deep and did not stand the test of time and events. We, however, are in the favorable position of a "second generation" assessment of that Islamic material. Our scholars and experts can report, in a detailed, authoritative way, on Islam within the Arabian Peninsula, on trends within Egyptian Islam, on the struggle between the Kemalist secular tradition in Turkey, and on the new Islamists, particularly the fight for the loyalty of European Islam between these who accept the canon, and the discipline, of modernism and those who don't.

Arabs and Muslims need not be believers in American exceptionalism, but our hope is to engage them in this contest of ideas. We will not necessarily aim at producing primary scholarship, but such scholarship may materialize in that our participants are researchers who know their subjects intimately. We see our critical output as essays accessible to a broader audience, primers about matters that require explication, op-eds, writings that will become part of the public debate, and short, engaging books that can illuminate the choices and the struggles in modern Islam.

We see this endeavor as a faithful reflection of the values that animate a decent, moderate society. We know the travails of modern Islam, and this working group will be unsparing in depicting them. But we also know that the battle for modern Islam is not yet lost, that there are brave men and women fighting to retrieve their faith from the extremists. Some of our participants will themselves be intellectuals and public figures who have stood up to the pressure. The working group will be unapologetic about America's role in the Muslim world. A power that laid to waste religious tyranny in Afghanistan and despotism in Iraq, that came to the rescue of the Muslims in the Balkans when they appeared all but doomed, has given much to those burdened populations. We haven't always understood Islam and Muslims —hence this inquiry. But it is a given of the working group that the pursuit of modernity and human welfare, and of the rule of law and reason, in Islamic lands is the common ground between America and contemporary Islam.

SAUDI ARABIA is an opaque country, making the access of researchers to its workings extremely limited. The 9/11 Commission Report acknowledged the opaqueness of that realm when it described the country as "a problematic ally in combating Islamic extremism." This strategic ally, the report reminds us, was the place where Al-Qaeda raised money for its activities and "the society that produced 15 of the 19 hijackers" who struck the United States on 9/11.

In the strategic landscape of the Persian Gulf and the eastern Mediterranean, Saudi Arabia is the leading Sunni Arab country in the standoff with Iran and a rival to the Persian revolutionary state. In the immediate Gulf neighborhood, and in Lebanon and the Palestinian territories, the will and the resources of Saudi Arabia are badly needed if the Iranian menace is to be met with a worthwhile regional challenger.

Joshua Teitelbaum has studied and followed the twists of Saudi Arabia's history and strategic choices for his entire academic career. A decade ago, he produced an authoritative monograph on the radical Islamists who stepped forth, in the aftermath of the Gulf War in 1990–1991, to challenge the House of Saud's political and religious legitimacy, *Holier than Thou: Saudi Arabia's Islamic Opposition* (2000). This new study rounds out his concerns, for it more directly takes up Saudi foreign policy in the Persian Gulf and in the Arab-Israeli peace process. Professor Teitelbaum provides a shrewd assessment of the Saudi-American relationship and a powerful corrective to the traditional view of Saudi foreign policy that emphasizes the Saudi concern with the Israeli-Palestinian conflict. The real play for Arabia's rulers is the ideological battle that has been opened up by Iran's push into Arab affairs. The country may be inaccessible, but the need for U.S. exposure to its politics and energy policies is more pressing than ever. This meticulous inquiry examines the way in which the Saudi rulers juggle the pressures and claims that intrude on their domain.

Fouad Ajami,
*Senior Fellow, Hoover Institution*
*Co-chairman, Herbert and Jane Dwight Working Group on Islamism and the International Order*

# Saudi Arabia and the New Strategic Landscape

## Joshua Teitelbaum

## INTRODUCTION

Two decades after the end of the Cold War, a new strategic landscape has appeared in the Middle East. No longer dominated by a U.S.-Soviet rivalry, this new landscape is dominated by U.S.-Iranian confrontation. In this struggle, the United States' most important Arab ally, Saudi Arabia, plays a key role. As the Obama administration policies allow Iran to run out the clock on getting a nuclear weapon, it would appear from its recent policy moves that it believes Riyadh is primarily concerned with the Arab-Israeli conflict. While this is a concern in Saudi Arabia, it is far and away not the primary one. Indeed, there is no doubt that in its foreign policy Riyadh is much more worried about Iran's rise as a key regional actor.

As a regional challenger, Iran threatens Saudi interests in Lebanon, where it operates with Syria and its Shiite proxy Hizballah to undermine the Saudi-supported government; in the Gaza Strip and the West Bank, where it supports the terrorist organization Hamas against the Palestinian Authority; in Yemen, where it is assisting rebels who are fighting the Saudi-supported regime of President Ali Abdallah Salih; and closer to home in the Persian Gulf, where it operates to curtail Saudi interests in Iraq and project its power into neighboring countries, particularly via their Shiite populations.

But the depth of Saudi Arabian concern about Iran goes beyond the basic regional balance of power or balance of threat considerations, reaching deep into the regime's calculus about its own security. This magnifies manyfold the importance to Saudi Arabia of confronting the Iranian-Shiite threat. Much of the regime's legitimacy comes from its role as the guardian of Sunni orthodoxy, the majority branch of Islam and the branch followed by most Saudi Arabians. This is a role felt keenly by the royal family, particularly the king, Abdallah bin Abd al-Aziz.[1] As the regime takes halting steps toward liberalization,[2] a rate of progress designed to mollify conservative forces within and without the royal family, Saudi Arabia's own minority Shiites, supported by Iran, push for greater rights within the kingdom. But the Sunni majority looks to the regime to uphold Sunni primacy at home and abroad. And important groups of Sunnis and Shiites call the rule of the Al Saud into question.

If Iran gets the upper hand, the royal family may face serious threats by Saudi Arabian Sunni radicals determined to stop the spread of Shiism, and by Saudi Arabian Shiites encouraged by the rise of Iran and its Shiite regional allies. Both sides would seek to exploit the situation, leading to instability in Saudi Arabia and reverberations of further regional instability.

# BACKGROUND: THE GENESIS OF SAUDI ARABIAN SECURITY CONCERNS

The Kingdom of Saudi Arabia has its origins in the mid-18th century, when an alliance was formed in the central Najd region between a local strongman, or emir, Muhammad bin Saud (d. 1765) of the Al Saud family, and a radical Islamic preacher, Shaykh Muhammad bin Abd al-Wahhab (1703–1791). A bargain was struck between these two ambitious men: Muhammad bin Abd al-Wahhab would give religious approbation for the expansionist desires of Muhammad bin Saud, and the latter would give the former the military force to spread his ideas of a more puritanical form of Islam than that which was practiced in the Arabian Peninsula. This alliance was successful and, despite various ups and downs, by 1932 the Al Saud had conquered most of the peninsula, including the relatively liberal and Islamically cosmopolitan Red Sea coastal area of the Hijaz, ruled by the Hashemite family,[3] with the holy cities of

4

Mecca and Medina, and Al-Hasa in the east, with its extensive Shiite population.

The formation of modern Saudi Arabia involved the subjugation of a diverse population—religiously, tribally, and regionally—to the whims of one family, the Al Saud. The royal family sought to identify itself with the state to such an extent that it named the state after itself—*Saudi* Arabia—one of only two states in the world named after a family.[4]

This subjugation came at a price. Although distribution of massive oil revenue has helped the Saudis to buy off much of the opposition over the years, it has not always been successful. Differing visions of Islam, from the Shiites of the eastern region of Al-Hasa to more liberal Islamists and extremist Wahhabis, who believe that the current regime is not extreme enough, have all challenged the rule of the Al Saud over the years. Underscoring all of this is the fact that the centralizing establishment of the Saudi state came at the expense of significant tribal autonomy. While discrete tribal loyalties have lost much of their political significance over the years because of the efforts of the Al Saud, the tribal ethos of a decentralized government and considerable tribal autonomy still presents a challenge to the regime and finds its expression in opposition movements.

One of the keenest historians of Saudi Arabia, Madawi Al-Rasheed, has observed: "The 20th century witnessed the emergence of a [Saudi Arabian] state imposed on people without a historical memory of unity or national heritage which would justify their inclusion in a single entity."[5] The security calculus of the Al Saud is therefore highly dominated by internal security concerns.

The Saudis have dealt with these domestic challenges in several ways. Tribal challengers were co-opted into the Saudi Arabian National Guard, which functioned essentially as a way to funnel oil rents to the tribes and buy their cooperation rather than as an effective fighting force. Sunni religious fanatics were given control of the religious establishment and the educational system, a move that would eventually backfire on the regime. The Shiites were ruthlessly suppressed, to the delight of the Sunni Wahhabi extremists who viewed Shiism as pure heresy.

External defense concerns have also been a significant part of Saudi security considerations. In the first years of the state, the descendants of the Hashemite family, recently ensconced by the British in Jordan and Iraq after being thrown out of the Hijaz by the Al Saud, sought to regain control of their ancestral homeland.[6] This led to the initial suspicion of the British and contributed to a bias toward the U.S. in the immediate post-World War II period. Indeed, in 1950 King Abd al-Aziz confided to U.S. Assistant Secretary of State George McGhee that the Hashemites were his greatest fear, and for that reason he wanted military aid and an urgent military alliance with America.[7]

American interest in Saudi Arabia dates from the 1930s with the development of oil. The desire to have access to oil outside the U.S. during World War II led the Roosevelt administration to declare in 1943 that "the defense of Saudi Arabia is vital to the defense of the United States," in order to provide Riyadh with Lend-Lease aid.[8]

# TWIN PILLARS: SAUDI ARABIA AND IRAN AS U.S. ALLIES IN THE PERSIAN GULF

Indeed, America's initial response to Saudi security concerns had more to do with oil than with the Hashemites. But the end of World War II brought the Cold War, which had an important Middle Eastern theater. Traditional Middle Eastern monarchies such as Jordan and Saudi Arabia sought to stymie Soviet Middle Eastern subversion, particularly through regional client states such as Egypt, Syria, Iraq, and Yemen.[9] For the Saudis, concerns about the Hashemites had given way to concerns over Communism. Early on the Saudis sought military support from the United States and received it through the United States Military Training Mission, established in 1953.

The Cold War coincided with increased development, education, and modernization in Saudi Arabia. This process brought with it some associated ills that affected internal security. Communist and Baathist cells were discovered, and labor unrest by Shiite workers in

Aramco's oil fields in the Eastern Province were frequent. These were cases of internal dissidents influenced by imported ideologies. The U.S. cooperated, with the help of Aramco, in keeping a lid on these developments.

Soviet encroachment and Arab radicalism were not the only Saudi external concerns. Across the Persian Gulf lay Iran. Saudi Arabia has always had an ambivalent relationship with Tehran. On the one hand, Iran, with its majority Shiite population, was deeply concerned about the establishment of anti-Shiite Wahhabi Saudi Arabia and what that would mean for access to holy places and for the fate of Saudi Arabia's sizable Shiite population. But aside from some minor friction, this did not develop into conflict. Religion was not a part of the shah's foreign policy.

More important, during this period Riyadh and Tehran were joined in their distrust of Communism and Soviet designs on the region. Iran, which had a border with the Soviet Union, had suffered years of Russian imperialism. The two countries even cooperated in the early 1970s to help the Sultan of Oman fight a

Maoist rebellion in the region of Dhofar. Both countries sought and received military equipment and training from a very willing United States. This policy earned the nickname "Twin Pillars" under the Nixon administration.[10]

The February 1979 Islamic Revolution in Iran and the December 1979 Soviet invasion of Afghanistan prompted President Jimmy Carter to announce what became known as the Carter Doctrine, during his January 1980 State of the Union address. Carter stressed that the

> Soviet effort to dominate Afghanistan has brought Soviet military forces to within 300 miles of the Indian Ocean and close to the Strait of Hormuz, a waterway through which most of the world's oil must flow. The Soviet Union is now attempting to consolidate a strategic position, therefore, that poses a grave threat to the free movement of Middle East oil.[11]

His conclusion was quite forceful:

> Let our position be absolutely clear: An attempt by any outside force to gain control of the Persian Gulf region will be regarded as an assault on

the vital interests of the United States of America, and such an assault will be repelled by any means necessary, including military force.[12]

The Carter Doctrine was given a specifically Saudi twist in October 1981, when President Ronald Reagan issued what has become known as the Reagan Corollary: "We cannot permit Saudi Arabia to become Iran," Reagan declared. The Carter Doctrine and the Reagan Corollary were responsible for the increase of the U.S. military presence in the Persian Gulf, first in the form of the Rapid Deployment Force, and eventually, a full military command, the U.S. Central Command.

The Reagan administration never lost hope that Iran could still be courted. Given the country's long border with the Soviet Union, the effort to return Iran to the fold was deemed too important to give up. The U.S. had an arms embargo against Iran, which had been embroiled in a war with Iraq since 1980 and was desperate for anti-tank and anti-aircraft missiles. In what became known as the Iran-Contra affair of the mid-1980s, the administration, with Israeli mediation, tried to trade arms to Tehran for U.S. hostages held by pro-Iranian Shiites in Lebanon. (Some of the funds from the sale of the missiles were diverted by Lt. Col. Oliver North of the National Security Council to the Contras in Nicaragua.) Secretary of State George Shultz had opposed the deal and was joined by Secretary of Defense Caspar Weinberger ("Cap Weinberger and George Shultz remained very much opposed, with Shultz especially strong in his opposition"[13]). But, the president, who had the support of CIA Director William Casey and national security adviser Robert McFarlane, overruled them both. Shultz had even threatened to resign, but Reagan convinced him otherwise, and was glad he had.[14]

According to Shultz, the Iran-Contra affair was an unnecessary distraction in relations with Iran. When Iran threatened Persian Gulf shipping in 1987 during the Iran-Iraq War, the U.S. led a reflagging effort, robustly confronting Iranian aggression. "After the setback wrought by the Iran-Contra affair," concluded Shultz, "Ronald Reagan was back in business."[15]

# A PILLAR COLLAPSES: FROM THE IRANIAN REVOLUTION TO THE END OF THE COLD WAR

1979 was a crucial year in the Persian Gulf. The Islamic Revolution ended decades of a pro-American regime in Tehran, and one that was more or less agnostic about Saudi Arabia. But unfortunately for the U.S. and Saudi Arabia, the new regime had a radical new agenda. It was not content dealing with internal affairs—it sought to export its revolution and to rectify perceived Western domination and oppression.

For Saudi Arabia, an ascendant, religiously based Iran presented new and unprecedented challenges. For the first time, a militant Shiite regime, flush with oil wealth, was poised across the Gulf from the Saudi guardian of Sunni orthodoxy. And the Iranians wasted little time.

*Shiite Riots in the Eastern Province and the Rise of Islamist Shiism in Saudi Arabia*

Iranian-inspired riots broke out toward the end of the year in the Shiite sections of Saudi

13

Arabia's oil-rich Eastern Province and continued into 1980, encouraged by the success of the Iranian Revolution. While the rioters had justifiable grievances based on years of Saudi discrimination, they also drew encouragement from the victories of fellow Shiites in Iran across the Gulf. The Saudi authorities used the Saudi Arabian National Guard to ruthlessly suppress the riots.[16] The government did not hesitate to use helicopter gunships against the demonstrators.[17] Many leaders of the Shiite community went into exile or were arrested following these protests.

The main Shiite opposition group, the Organization of the Islamic Revolution (*Munazzamat al-Thawra al-Islamiyya*), was established by Shaykh Hasan al-Saffar, a Shiite cleric, in December 1979, following the first burst of rioting. The group functioned as a political and religious outlet for feelings of oppression and insult.[18]

Saffar was echoing the thoughts of Ayatollah Ruhollah Khomeini when he wrote:

> . . . we are genuinely part of the realm of the downtrodden [*mustad'afun*] while the despots of

Al Saʻud . . . are genuinely part of the realm of oppressors . . . and colonizers. The ongoing battle is now between these two realms. . . . Our struggle against . . . tyrannical rule is a cycle of a long chain of a universal revolution which will, inevitably, lead to the collapse of imperialistic superpowers and the rise of the world of the downtrodden. . . .[19]

After the uprising Saffar found asylum in Iran, and his organization established offices in Tehran, London, and Washington.

## *Making Trouble in Lebanon: Iran and the Rise of Hizballah*

As it spread its revolutionary Islamist message throughout the Middle East, Iran put a special emphasis on the Shiite population of Lebanon, which was the largest but poorest and least-represented sector of Lebanon's intricate confessional framework. It was involved with the precursors of the radical terrorist organization Hizballah, which struck twice in Beirut in 1983, bombing the U.S. Embassy (63 killed) in April and the Marine barracks (241 killed) in October. Hizballah, whose leader, Hasan Nasrallah, is a follower of Iranian Supreme Leader Ali Khamenei, would grow to be a powerful force in Lebanon.

Saudi Arabia's efforts to negotiate an end to the Lebanese Civil War finally bore fruit in an agreement signed in the Saudi city of Taif in 1989, which sought to more fairly distribute power in Lebanon. But it regularized the Syrian presence in the country and allowed Hizballah to maintain its arms, ostensibly to confront Israel. Thus Iran's presence in Lebanon was made final by the official recognition of the status of its allies Syria and Hizballah.

*Wahhabi Extremists on the Offensive*

On the Sunni scene in Saudi Arabia, the years of catering to Wahhabi extremists of various kinds were beginning to be felt. As it will be remembered, the Al Saud had given control of the mosque network and educational system to the Wahhabi establishment, which preached an extreme puritanical and anti-Western doctrine.

In exchange, the theory went, religious leaders would give approbation for the modernization of the state and look the other way at the sometimes "un-Islamic" behavior of the royal family. But this bargain was not working out as expected.[20]

Sunni Islamic extremists took over the Grand Mosque in Mecca nearly simultaneously with the Shiite uprising of 1979, protesting what they saw as the lax Islamic system in Saudi Arabia and the un-Islamic behavior of the royal family. They held out for two weeks.[21] Both events demonstrated the difficulties of Saudi internal security and their connection to regional developments.

The regime decided to deal with Wahhabi extremism in a unique way. First, it joined the Wahhabi religious establishment in encouraging Saudi youth to travel to Afghanistan to fight the Soviets after their 1979 invasion. The idea was essentially to "export" violent extremists and—the regime hoped—have them "martyred" overseas. This dovetailed nicely with the cooperative U.S. and Saudi efforts to confront the Soviet Union in the last decade of the Cold

War. The other aspect of dealing with the problem of homegrown Islamist extremists was to export their zeal and money overseas to the West, where they could preach their doctrine at local mosques, often built with money from the Saudi royal family. In this manner, it was believed, these forces could be co-opted and their energy could be channeled to foreign lands.

The main regional story of the Persian Gulf in the 1980s was the Iran-Iraq War (1980–1988). Iraq sought to exploit Iranian internal turmoil and expand its narrow territory along the Persian Gulf. In its rhetoric, Baghdad, drawing on Islamic history, portrayed its attack as defending the Arab east from the predations of Persian Shiites. Saddam Hussein was widely supported by the Arab states of the Gulf, fearful of the implications of an ascendant Iran.

This was a time of extreme tension between Saudi Arabia and Iran. Iran saw Saudi Arabia as trying to undermine the Islamic Revolution by supporting Iraqi aggression, while Saudi Arabia suffered from Iranian agitation and even violence during the annual pilgrimage (*hajj*) in Mecca. For many years, the Iranians used the pilgrimage as an arena of confrontation with the pro-Western Al Saud, holding protests and encouraging rioting that sometimes resulted in the loss of life.[22]

## THE NEW STRATEGIC LANDSCAPE

Needless to say, the collapse of the Soviet Union in 1991 did not mean the end of security challenges for the United States and Saudi Arabia. All it did was create a new strategic landscape with different challenges. Saudi concerns became more focused on the growing strength of Iran, and the implications that this would have on Riyadh's position in the region and the effect of this new position on domestic security.

By August 1990, Saddam Hussein had turned his aggression from Iran to Kuwait. Within days of capturing the small Gulf nation, Iraqi troops were poised on the Kuwaiti-Saudi border. The U.S. sprang into action, sending hundreds of thousands of troops to defend the kingdom. Extremist Wahhabis were outraged, as they could not stomach the idea that Christian unbelievers were defending them. This was the start of an active movement of Sunni Saudi Arabian opposition.[23] The most violent trend in this movement was headed by Usama bin Ladin.

The Saudi regime's support of the Afghan jihad was key to the development of the Sunni opposition in Saudi Arabia. Thousands of young men gained military experience in Afghanistan. Whey they returned home, they were ready to turn their jihadi energies inward, and Usama bin Ladin was there to guide them. In November 1995, Saudi sons of the Afghan jihad blew up the Riyadh headquarters of the U.S. Office of the Program Manager—Saudi Arabian National Guard, which supported the National Guard's modernization program. Seven people were killed, including five U.S. citizens, and 42 others were seriously injured.[24]

Iranian subversion in Saudi Arabia reached its peak in June 1996, when Iranian-backed Saudi Shiites blew up Khobar Towers in Dhahran, a complex housing U.S. Air Force personnel from the 4404th Fighter Wing (Provisional) and troops from the U.K. and France enforcing the United Nations-sponsored "no-fly" zone in southern Iraq. All 19 people killed in the explosion were U.S. servicemen, and nearly 500 U.S. and other personnel were injured.[25] Although the Iranian link was clear to the Saudis and the Americans—the Justice Department's June 2001 indictment accused "elements of the Iranian government" but did not name them[26]—neither the Clinton administration nor the successor Bush administration took action against Iran.

For the Saudis, who, after much prodding, had helped develop the evidence against Iran, the lack of a firm American response led them to believe they had discovered a hard truth: The U.S. could not be depended upon to confront Iranian aggression. Fearing further Iranian aggression and knowing that they could not count on the U.S., the Saudis chose to cut a deal with Iran. It would not provide the U.S. with conclusive, prosecutable evidence of Iranian involvement, and Iran would refrain from supporting terrorist activity in Saudi Arabia. This wary rapprochement has held, for the time being.

The Saudi policy of exporting its homemade brand of extremist Islam overseas in order to make it someone else's problem had horrifying results: the terrorist atrocities against the U.S. that took place on September 11, 2001. Fifteen of the 19 hijackers were Saudis, protégés of the Saudi leader of Al-Qaeda, Usama bin Ladin.

In a sense, the chickens had come home to roost. Years of unchecked funding of Islamic extremism, including by members of the Saudi royal family and their associates, had led to a terrible outrage. Tension developed in the U.S.-Saudi relationship as aspects of this support became clear. "If I could somehow snap my fingers and cut off the funding from one country, it would be Saudi Arabia," Stuart Levey, the undersecretary of the Treasury in charge of tracking terror financing, told ABC News on the sixth anniversary of the attacks.[27] Both sides soon realized that they had a common enemy in Sunni Islamic extremism and that they needed each other's help.

As the Saudis surveyed their strategic situation after 9/11, they saw two main challenges. The first was internal Sunni terrorism. They knew that the "success" of 9/11 gave encouragement to radical Islamists inside Saudi Arabia, where Bin Ladin was widely popular.[28] And after all, Bin Ladin had made it clear that his target was not only the West, but also Muslim leaders who trucked with it, and in particular the Saudi royal family. The second was an ascendant Iran.

The U.S. invasion of Iraq in March 2003 had implications for both of these Saudi security challenges, and it was a mixed blessing. On the one hand, it took out Saddam Hussein, one of the Saudis' biggest enemies, who had been poised to attack the country in 1990. Yet on the other hand, by removing Iraq from the Arab-Iranian balance of power in the Persian Gulf, the U.S. had played into the hands of Iran, which was delighted to see the end of the notorious Baath regime that had carried out the unprovoked attack in 1980 and had oppressed and murdered Iraqi Shiites.

Saudi jihadists began to flow across the border to participate in the jihad against the U.S. and the ascendant Shiite majority. The best that could be said about this was that the Saudi authorities were turning a blind eye.[29] U.S. military sources believed that Saudis were the largest foreign contingent of insurgents, and that they were being funded by Saudi sources.[30] The reason was clear: The Saudis wanted to prevent a Shiite regime sympathetic to Iran taking over in Iraq.

The year 2003 was also the beginning of a serious Al-Qaeda insurgency within Saudi Arabia. There were several attacks lasting into 2007, when they became less numerous as Saudi counterinsurgency efforts grew more effective. Yet new arrests are constantly being made, and sporadic attacks continue to occur.[31] In fact, a daring attack occurred on August 28, 2009, when a suicide bomber got close enough to slightly wound Prince Muhammad bin Naif Al Saud. Prince Muhammad, the man largely responsible for fighting the insurgency, is the son of Prince Naif, minister of the interior and third in line to the Saudi throne.[32] The incident was unprecedented and proof that the Al-Qaeda-led insurgency in Saudi Arabia was not dead.

Saudi Arabia has received a lot of credit, and probably deservedly so, for its effort to deprogram Islamic extremists and rehabilitate them.[33] The recidivism rate seems to be low, and the rate of attacks has dropped.[34] Still, the program has been criticized by Amnesty International, which has accused the kingdom of holding more than 3,000 suspects in secret detention and torturing many of them.[35] The rehabilitation effort is based on tribal principles of personal contact, mediation, and generosity. Top Saudi officials are in contact with the terrorists and their families, promising that they will be treated fairly and given financial advantages such as a car and the forgiving of debts.[36] The limitations of this approach were seen in the suicide bombing attack against Prince Muhammad. The terrorist had returned from Yemen and was on the prince's private plane, and the prince was expecting him. The bomb was concealed on or in the terrorist's body.[37]

It bears stressing that Iran has its hand in the Sunni opposition as well as in the Shiite one. Saudi officials, who released a list of 85 of its most-wanted Sunni terrorists, noted that 35 of them were last seen in Iran.[38]

The Sunni extremist insurgency within Saudi Arabia is certainly a major challenge to the regime, which seems to have handled it fairly well, if one is to judge by the drop in terrorist incidents. But it is really only the extreme end of a deeper problem, and that is one of the legitimacy of the current regime. While most of the opponents of the regime do not turn to violence, many question whether the regime is being true to Islam as perceived by the Wahhabi founders. Although King Abdallah is widely viewed as a liberalizing monarch, he is painfully aware that the Wahhabi establishment and more extremist Wahhabis are watching him. He therefore balances his liberalizing steps with more conservative ones such as temporarily shutting down newspapers believed to have published unsuitable material.

There is a debate within Saudi Arabia, including within the royal family, about how to maintain a conservative country in a constantly globalizing world where information knows no borders.[39] Saudi Arabia tries to censor the

Internet, but it knows that its efforts are little more than a finger in the dike.[40] Saudi Arabia has recently established the King Abdallah University of Science and Technology, a research university in Jeddah where there will be coeducational classes and the curriculum will be free of the influence of Wahhabi conservatives. When a high-ranking cleric from the Senior Ulama Council, Shaykh Saad al-Shithri, questioned the propriety of women and men studying together, he was promptly relieved of his duties by the king.[41] It seems clear that King Abdallah has a vision of a moderately conservative Islamic country that maintains tradition while making progress, but he is careful not to offend the conservative elements of his society. This will make for very slow progress, but only the Saudis can determine its pace.

*Iran in the New Strategic Landscape: Challenging Saudi Arabia Regionally and Domestically*

In the 30 years since the Islamic Revolution, Iran has formed anti-American alliances with states (Syria and Venezuela[42]) and non-state actors (Hizballah, Hamas, and groups in Yemen[43]). It supported Shiite terrorism in Bahrain, Kuwait, Lebanon, and Saudi Arabia, and most recently in Saudi ally Egypt, via its Hizballah proxy.[44] The removal of Saddam Hussein's regime in Iraq in 2003 and the meteoric rise in the price of oil further strengthened Iran's hand. Hizballah's victories in internal Lebanese politics and its bloodying of Israel in the 2006 Second Lebanon War (known as the July War in Lebanon) could all be viewed as increasing Iran's prestige, to the detriment of the U.S. position in the region, as well as to that of Saudi Arabia.

Let there be no doubt, Saudi Arabia is a stable country. The government has proven itself adept at handling internal challenges. The Al Saud is very keen on keeping it that way, although these challenges remain potent. The new strategic *regional* landscape, characterized by an ascendant Iran, therefore has direct implications for *domestic* security in Saudi Arabia. These domestic security challenges come from both the majority Sunni population and the minority Shiites.

Neither of these security challenges is new. But the rise of the Iranian-Shiite threat has exacerbated them and added a new internal dimension to what might have been only a regional problem. A nuclear-armed Iran would certainly be the crowning glory of Iranian efforts for regional domination, at the expense of the West and its local allies.

With respect to the majority Sunnis, much of the regime's legitimacy stems from its position internationally as the defender of Sunni orthodoxy against the perceived heresy of the Shiites, who left the orthodox fold in the seventh century. The success of Iran and its proxies in Lebanon, the Gaza Strip, and Iraq raised an alarm among many Sunnis in Saudi Arabia. To them, it seems that the thousand-year-old status quo in the Islamic world is being turned upside down, and that those who are following the "true" Islamic path are being defeated. Sunni websites in Saudi Arabia as well as the printed press in the Arab world have called attention to the dangers.[45]

As we have seen, the Iranian-Shiite ascendancy has caused alarm among the majority Sunni population and concern among leading clerics and the royal family. The Sunnis are the bedrock of the regime's legitimacy, founded as it was, it will be remembered, on the basis of an extremist Sunni ideology, Wahhabism. But the rise of Iran and its Shiite proxies has emboldened Saudi Arabia's own Shiite population, which makes its home in the oil-rich Eastern Province.

There can be no doubt that the most significant recent event for Saudi Shiites was the downfall of Saddam Hussein in April 2003. The Shiites felt empowered—even emboldened. Najaf, the holy shrine and the heart of Shiism, had been liberated. Seeing millions of their Iraqi brethren freely carrying out the holy rituals of Ashura, they felt their time had now come within Saudi Arabia—a Shiite state in Iraq would bring Saudi Shiites their due. One Shiite religious official, who preferred to remain anonymous, told a reporter: "If a Shia state takes place in Iraq, we can be assured that there will be justice. It will be based on the religious teachings of the prophet, and after that, the Saudi Shia will be in a better situation." In an uncharacteristically public move, Shiite leaders expressed their satisfaction with the end of the Baath regime, but followed their expression of happiness with a call to improve their own situation. The leading Shiite figure, Shaykh Hasan al-Saffar, said that now Saudi Shiites were "determined to claim some of their rights while defending the nation's unity."[46]

The Shiite ascendancy, which became evident in Iraq during 2005 and into 2006, increased tension between Sunnis and Shiites in the kingdom. Egyptian President Husni Mubarak's remarks in March 2005 that Shiites were more loyal to Iran than to their own countries elicited a flood of protests from Saudi Shiites, particularly because no one in the Saudi government found it necessary to contradict Mubarak and attest to the loyalty of Saudi Shiites. But the perception on the part of Saudi Sunnis that Saudi Shiites were more loyal to Iran was very widespread, according to leading Saudi liberal Turki al-Hamad. "I'd say 90 percent of the people in Saudi Arabia don't trust the Shiites," he said.[47]

The 2006 war in Lebanon, during which Hizballah attacked the Israeli home front with seeming impunity and appeared triumphant, only worsened matters for Saudi Shiites. While King Abdallah had been ready to publicly meet with Shiites, Hizballah's popularity in the Arab world together with the destabilization of the pro-Saudi government in Lebanon were more than he could bear. The government came out strongly against Hizballah and Iran, calling Hizballah's kidnapping of two Israeli soldiers "rash adventures carried out by elements inside the state and those behind them." At the same time, there were pro-Hizballah demonstrations in the Eastern Province.[48] With this background, King Abdallah was not able—or did not want—to restrain the traditional Wahhabi anti-Shiite polemics from bursting forth. At a time of Shiite ascendancy, the leading Sunni state could not be seen as coddling the Shiites.

The prominence of Hizballah during the July 2006 war led to a discussion of the organization in particular, and by implication the Shiites in general, as well as the Shiites in Saudi Arabia. Safar al-Hawali, once of the opposition "Awakening Shaykhs" who became popular in the 1990s and still maintained his distance from the regime, castigated Hizballah (which means "party of God") as "Hizb al-Shaytan" ("party of Satan"), and said that it was forbidden to pray for it or to support it in any way. His former partner in the opposition of the 1990s, but who now was closer to the regime, Shaykh Salman al-Awda, exhibited a more Arab nationalist bent, saying that while there were disputes with the Shiites, "I, as a Muslim and an Arab, feel happy when Hizballah inflicts damage on the Zionists, and we should praise the resistance in the media."[49] The dividing line between the two former oppositionists was clear: Hawali had boycotted the 2003 Saudi National Dialogue with the Shiites, while Awda had attended.

Extremist Wahhabi shaykhs continued to point out the "evil nature" of the Shiites. During the Lebanon War, a fatwa appeared on the Internet by leading Sunni Shaykh Abdallah bin Jibrin, a former member of the establishment Senior Ulama Council, calling on Sunnis to disavow Hizballah as a party of heretical anti-Sunni troublemakers.[50] Although Bin Jibrin later said this was an old fatwa that was no longer applicable to the present situation,[51] his anti-Shiite views were well known, and he had even called for killing Shiites in a fatwa he published in 1991.[52]

Websites run by less established but popular clerics published virulently anti-Shiite polemics. The Nur al-Islam website even had a page dedicated to articles on the subject, titled, "the Rawafid [a derogatory Sunni term for Shiites, meaning 'those who reject Islam'] are Coming," and illustrated it with bloody graphics.[53] Shiite websites castigated Bin Jibrin, warning him not to forget that he would have to face God on judgment day. The radical Saudi Shiite Hizballah al-Hijaz issued a statement saying that Bin Jibrin had angered "all the sons of the Arabian Peninsula, not to mention the entire Islamic nation. This occurs while the Islamic nation is at the peak of its feelings of pride, dignity, and joys of victory over the sons of Zion, the victory that is recorded by the hand of the mujahidin of Lebanon's Hizballah."[54]

The intensification of Sunni-Shiite strife in Iraq was reflected in a fatwa signed by 38 radical Sunni ulama in December 2006. Although it was addressed to the Sunnis of Iraq as a message of support, it was strongly anti-Shiite in general, complaining about their un-Islamic practices. This fatwa had been organized by Shaykh Abd al-Rahman al-Barrak, a radical cleric who occasionally could be seen on official Saudi TV.[55] Barrak also issued his own fatwa, which proclaimed the infidelity (*takfir*) of the Shiites and their polytheistic practices, and repeated the old accusation that a Jew had founded the sect.[56] In January 2007, Bin Jibrin let his true colors fly, and published a fatwa on his own website giving eight reasons why the Shiites should be considered polytheists (*mushrikin*). He distinguished between the Shiites and "true Muslims."[57]

For the Saudi Shiites who supported a model of cooperation with the regime, Shiite identification with Hizballah proved particularly problematic. Saudi Arabia is a Sunni religious state. To identify with a Shiite movement and, by implication, the Shiite state of Iran ran counter to the normative Saudi ethos. As time wore on and Shiite regional ascendancy became more apparent, Shaykh Salman al-Awda sounded the alarm about Sunni conversion to Shiism (*tash-ayyu*'), expressing his fear that Shiite victories in Lebanon and Iraq might draw Sunnis away.[58] Many Saudi newspapers carried warnings from Wahhabi clerics against conversion to Shiism.[59] King Abdallah himself addressed this issue in an interview with the Kuwaiti newspaper *Al-Siyasa* in late January 2007. The interviewer referred to a "campaign" of Shiite proselytism and asked what was Saudi Arabia's position on the issue as the source of religious emulation (*marja*') for Muslims and protector of the law of God and his creed. King Abdallah, accepting the premise of the question regarding the campaign and Saudi Arabia's role as protector of the Sunnis, said that the Saudi leadership was following the issue, but that the attempt would fail because Sunnis held fast to their beliefs.[60] The presentation of Saudi Arabia as the source of religious emulation for Muslims drew a stark distinction between Shiite Iran and Sunni Wahhabi Saudi Arabia.

The regime is caught between its Wahhabi roots and wishes by some in the royal family, particularly King Abdallah, to effect reconciliation with the Shiites. A graphic illustration of this dilemma is shown in examples from two websites: A Saudi Sunni rabidly anti-Shiite website, Al-Furqan, published a "document" stating that according to Shiite calculations, King Abdallah would be killed on December 18, 2007, which is one month before the coming of the Shiite Mahdi, or messiah.[61] On the other hand, the Shiite Al-Rasid site published a tongue-in-cheek article titled "King Abdallah is a Shiite," which expressed support for Abdallah, as if to say that since even the king respected Shiite rights, there was no reason to question the loyalty of Saudi Arabia's Shiite citizens.[62]

The Sunni-Shiite confrontation on the Internet continues unabated. In May 2007 Sunni activists hacked Hasan al-Saffar's website and published the following message: "In the name of God, the Merciful and Compassionate: All heretical Shiite websites will be attacked and all sites belonging to the Majus [pagan Zoroastrians, a reference to Iran] will be removed from the Internet."[63]

In general, over the years there has been some improvement in the lot of the Shiites of Saudi Arabia. They are allowed to hold Ashura commemorations, publish Shiite works, and open Shiite mosques and schools, albeit all in a very slow and highly scrutinized manner.[64] Even so, Saudi Shiites never stop worrying that their hard-won gains may evaporate one day and they do not have faith in the government. Paradoxically, the gains of their Iraqi brethren might cause them to lose some of what they have achieved in Saudi Arabia. Saudi Sunnis accuse Saudi Shiites of funding terrorism against Sunnis in Iraq,[65] while Saudi Shiites accuse Saudi Sunnis of funneling funds to Sunni terrorists in Iraq. Saudi Shiites are also worried about extremists in their midst. In the village of Awwamiya, some residents were reported to be carrying automatic weapons and wearing necklaces with a picture of Hizballah Secretary-General Hasan Nasrallah.[66]

In order to preserve their gains, the Shiites seem to believe that it is necessary for King Abdallah to speak out against anti-Shiite fatwas; indeed, they argue that such fatwas should be criminalized.[67] Otherwise, they maintain, matters run the danger of returning to the problematic 1980s. But it is likely that they will be disappointed. Relations between the regime and the Shiite population are fraught with difficulty. Given the reliance of the regime on the Sunni Wahhabi clerics, it is unlikely that they will rein in their fatwas. The situation in Iraq has made it much harder to do so. The royal family feels keenly its role as a leader of the Sunni world, and local Sunnis are pressuring the regime to support the Sunnis in Iraq. In the face of the regional Shiite ascendancy marked by Hizballah's performance against Israel, a possible Shiite state in Iraq, and a powerful Iran, it is likely that Saudi Shiites will continue to pay the price of being the ultimate "other," sacrificed on the altar of the Wahhabi legitimacy on which the regime is so dependent.

Sunni-Shiite tensions in Saudi Arabia are not caused by Iran and the Shiite ascendancy in the region, but they are certainly exacerbated by them. While King Abdallah has tried to mollify both Saudi Shiites and Sunnis, the successes of Iran and its proxies make this a very difficult task. If the regime is soft on Iran regionally and on its own Shiites domestically, it risks an increased challenge from Sunni extremists disappointed in the Al Saud's failure to stop the march of Shiism. And if Iran continues its successes, it will further embolden Saudi Shiites, thus raising tensions with Saudi Sunnis, all to the detriment of the royal family. In this manner, the new strategic landscape, characterized by the rise of Iran, has profound implications for Saudi domestic security.

In Lebanon, the latest setback to Saudi regional dominance began with the assassination of a popular Saudi protégé, Prime Minister Rafiq al-Hariri, in February 2005. Iran's ally Syria was widely believed to be behind the attack. While a blow to Saudi regional prestige, the attack led to what became known as the Cedar Revolution and later the March 14 Movement, which forced the Syrians to withdraw their troops from Lebanon, although a major intelligence presence remained. But Hizballah, Syria and Iran's main ally, remains strong and carries considerable influence in Lebanese politics. Iran's position in Lebanon thus remains equally strong, to the chagrin of the Saudis.

In the Palestinian arena, Iran continued to stymie Saudi policy. Riyadh, concerned about the terrorist Hamas organization's gains at the expense of the more moderate Palestinian Authority, headed by President Mahmud Abbas, negotiated the Mecca Agreement between the two factions in February 2007. However, it was soon torn up by Hamas, which took sole control of the Gaza Strip from Abbas' Fatah faction after bloody fighting. Iran's hand in the Hamas victory was clear, thus handing the Saudis another regional defeat.

In addition to Lebanon, Palestine, and Iraq, Yemen has presented a relatively new theater of Saudi-Iranian conflict. In what has the definite look of a proxy war, Saudi Arabia is supporting Yemen against a rebellion of Zaydi Shiites (known as Huthis after their leader, Husayn Badr al-Din al-Huthi) in its northern province of Sada. There have been several rounds of fighting since June 2004. A great deal of circumstantial evidence points to Iranian support for the Huthis. One Huthi cleric has even stated that he and other clerics have studied in Iran and support Iranian Shiism. Moreover, along with Hizballah's Hasan Nasrallah, the Hawthi leadership considers Iranian Supreme Leader Ali Khamenei to be its source of religious emulation.[68]

Saudi Arabia is trying to prevent Iran from gaining a foothold in Yemen, which sits strategically at the confluence of the Red Sea and the Gulf of Aden, facing the Horn of Africa. Yemen is already the cross-border base for Al-Qaeda's Saudi Arabian branch, which has melded with the Yemeni branch of the organization. Moreover, Sada borders the southern Saudi province of Najran, which has a significant Isma'ili Shiite minority that has on occasion protested its second-class status.

The Yemeni government and the Saudi press have accused Iran of arming and funding the rebels. The Saudi satellite station, Al-Arabiyya, broadcasted a report on "the Al-Huthi rebellion and Iran's role in it." Saudi officials have said that they are coordinating efforts with the Yemenis and have, in unattributed comments, accused Iran of supporting the rebels. Support for the Huthis has been shown on Hizballah's website and on Iranian television.[69] Iran's minister of Foreign Affairs, Manouchehr Mottaki, has expressed "deep concern for the situation of the Shiites in Yemen." Iranian media have even reported that the Saudi Arabian air force has been involved in the bombing of rebel strongholds.[70]

Toward the end of October 2009 the war of words heated up. The Huthis accused the Saudis of using heavy machine-gun fire against a northern Yemeni border town. In Tehran, Iranian students protested at the Saudi Embassy against the reported Saudi action.[71] In early November, the rebels said they had seized mountainous territory inside Saudi Arabia, and Saudi authorities said gunmen crossing from Yemen had killed a security officer.[72]

Further evidence of Iranian designs can be implied from Iran's increase of its naval presence in the Gulf of Aden, ostensibly to combat piracy. Israel is concerned that Iran, by advancing political and economic interests in Sudan,

Eritrea, and Djibouti, will increase and maintain an active military in the Red Sea and threaten the Jewish state.[73]

While the Obama administration has sought to link progress on the Israeli-Arab conflict with a solution to the Iranian nuclear issue, they are in fact separate issues. Indeed, the normalization required of the Arabs as part of an Arab-Israeli deal presents Saudi Arabia in particular with a host of internal legitimacy issues. On the other hand, Saudi Arabians are increasingly worried about Iran, as demonstrated by recent polls, which show a huge jump from 27 percent in 2008 to 47 percent in 2009 of Saudi Arabians who believe that Iran should be pressured to give up its nuclear program. Fifty-two percent of Saudis believe that Iran is intent on getting nuclear weapons. In a 2007 poll, 38 percent of Saudis favored the U.S. and other countries taking military action against Iran if diplomacy failed to stop the development of nuclear weapons.[74]

The Iranian nuclear program is already fueling an effort by Arab Gulf countries to begin their own nuclear effort. According to a report in the *Guardian*, in 2003 the Saudis were considering such an effort to counter Iran. Among the paths being considered was the purchase of a nuclear warhead. Another option was to seek nuclear protection from another country. Indeed, on more than one occasion U.S. Secretary of State Hillary Clinton has suggested an American nuclear umbrella.[75]

Recently, the United Arab Emirates has begun negotiations for an agreement on the civilian use of nuclear technology with the United States. This is a worrisome trend, and it is hard to fathom the thinking behind the Bush administration, which was negotiating this development. Several experts on nonproliferation have questioned the civilian applications of nuclear technology for an energy-rich country such as the U.A.E. Joe Cirincione, president of the anti-nuclear weapons Ploughshares Fund, stated: "I have a hard time believing that Middle East leaders got together to watch Al Gore's movie and decided to reduce their carbon footprint. This is not about energy. It is about Iran."[76]

It is clear that for both domestic and regional reasons, Saudi Arabia wants to see the

Iran nuclear problem disappear. It will be remembered that in the aftermath of the 1996
Khobar Towers bombing of U.S. troops, Riyadh was reluctant to provide the U.S. with the
smoking gun that would permit it to retaliate
against Iran, because it was unsure of how consistent and forceful the U.S. response would be.
Instead, it chose to mollify Iran. Now, more
than a decade later, Iran is on the brink of a
nuclear weapons breakthrough. Saudi Arabia
awaits a robust U.S. response. Meanwhile, reports that Saudi Arabia has given Israel a secret
nod to cross its territory should it decide to attack Iran do not seem so far-fetched.[77]

Amid several mysterious reports of various
efforts to disrupt the Iranian nuclear program,
mostly attributed to the Mossad,[78] Saudi Arabia, perhaps with the cooperation of the United
States, seems also to be doing its fair share. In
late May, while on pilgrimage to Saudi Arabia,
Iranian nuclear scientist Shahram Amiri disap-
peared.[79] Although Saudi officials do not com-
ment on the Iranian nuclear issue, the Saudi
press has become more vocal in the past year.

For example, in an October 2009 editorial, *Al-Sharq al-Awsat* editor Tariq al-Humayd raised serious questions about Iran's intentions.[80] He further accused Tehran of abetting terrorism and inciting Shiite-Sunni sectarian strife. The daily *Al-Watan* took Iran to task for destabilizing Yemen, Lebanon, Palestine, and Iraq. It termed those who defended Iran "filthy writers and spokesmen."[81]

Although Saudi-Iranian confrontations around the annual pilgrimage have tapered off since the mid-1990s, tension rose again as the pilgrimage approached in late November 2009. The cause was the threat to Saudi interests, both domestic and regional, by Iran. In late October, Iranian President Mahmoud Ahmadinejad issued a veiled threat to Saudi Arabia, warning it against harming Iranian pilgrims. Iran signaled that it might return to the old policy of using the pilgrimage as an occasion to hold demonstrations condemning "infidels" (read the United States). The Saudi press warned against the "desecration" of the pilgrimage, and the country's top religious official, Shaykh

Abd al-Aziz Al al-Shaykh, said that such demonstrations were not Islamic. Amid Iranian reports that Iranian pilgrims were being detained unnecessarily at Medina airport, the Saudi cabinet issued a warning to pilgrims not to demonstrate during the annual ritual.[82]

Gulf Cooperation Council countries such as Kuwait, Saudi Arabia, and Bahrain, which have significant Shiite populations, have been jittery about Iran for years. (Bahrain is ruled by Sunnis but has a Shiite majority.) Recently the U.A.E., which has a territorial dispute with Iran over three Persian Gulf islands, reportedly uncovered a plot by Iran to blow up the tallest building in the world, Burj Dubai. Reports to this effect appeared in the Israeli and Kuwaiti press in mid-September. They were denied by Dubai authorities.[83]

## THE U.S. AND SAUDI SECURITY: FAILING TO UNDERSTAND THE NEW STRATEGIC LANDSCAPE

U.S. administrations are not accustomed to delving into the internal problems of allies. The view has often been that these allies know what is best for themselves, and the traditional goal of America, as the superpower-protector, is to protect the ally from external enemies, unless specifically asked to help put down a domestic insurgency. The Saudi leadership is well-educated and familiar with American culture and the ways of Washington. The Saudi envoy to the U.S., Ambassador Adel Al-Jubeir, a protégé of King Abdallah, is a good example of the leadership, having spent nearly 25 years in the U.S. after being schooled at the University of North Texas and Georgetown University. Saudi leaders know how to talk to the American leadership, although they tend not to talk about domestic issues. What concerns us the most, the Saudis say, is the Arab-Israeli conflict.

The Obama administration has once again taken the Saudis at their word and placed the Arab-Israeli conflict at the top of its agenda, when it should be playing second fiddle to the Iranian threat. But the U.S. should know by now that the Saudis are notoriously circumspect about discussing their real fears: an ascendant Iran and its implications for their domestic stability. Until 9/11, and to its detriment, the U.S. relied solely on Saudi interlocutors for information on Saudi internal matters. The U.S. was assured that everything was under control. That is one reason 9/11 was such a surprise.

A similar situation exists now. The Saudis are supremely concerned about an ascendant Iran (along with a Shiite-dominated Iraq) and its implications for its own domestic stability. This increases by several orders of magnitude a simple threat by a regional rival. By not understanding the close connection between a strong Iran and Saudi domestic concerns, the U.S. risks underestimating the magnitude of the Iranian threat to the Saudis.

Only a comprehensive and deep understanding of the complexity of Saudi domestic and regional concerns can really inform American decision-makers confronted with the new strategic landscape in the Middle East. The current administration seems woefully misinformed, as it has devoted the bulk of its Middle East efforts to the Arab-Israeli conflict. While pursuing an Arab-Israeli peace is a worthy goal, history has demonstrated that progress is made only when the sides are ripe for progress, and they are not yet. Romantic notions of making peace in the Holy Land have often foundered on the rocks of misguided policies and over-eager American administrations from both political parties.

President Barack Obama has sought to build on the Saudi-sponsored Arab Peace Initiative of 2002 in order to jump-start the Middle East peace process. In the wake of the terrorist attacks of September 11, 2001, Saudi Arabia was under intense scrutiny because 15 of the 19 hijackers had proved to be Saudis. In February 2002, Crown Prince Abdullah of Saudi Arabia gave an interview to *New York Times* columnist Thomas Friedman in which he proposed to Israel "full withdrawal from all the occupied territories, in accord with U.N. resolutions, including in Jerusalem, for full normalization of relations." In a flash, Abdullah had transformed the discourse: Instead of focusing on Saudi involvement in terrorism, the Western press was now talking about Saudi peacemaking. This clever move shifted the onus onto Israel.[84]

The Saudis agreed to a severely hardened version of the plan at a March 2002 meeting of the Arab League, where the Arabs rejected any settlement of the Palestinian refugees in the Arab countries. Moreover, Riyadh made it clear that the plan was not open for negotiation and was in fact a take-it-or-leave-it proposal. Saudi Foreign Minister Saud al-Feisal stressed: "This initiative is an indivisible whole, and consequently it is impossible to accept one part of it and refuse another." He added that the Arabs "now have a weapon to put pressure on Israel on the international scene and even on public opinion in Israel."[85]

But the Obama administration seems intent on finessing the Saudi plan. In an announcement at the State Department appointing George Mitchell as special envoy for Middle East peace, the president stated that "the Arab peace initiative contains constructive elements that could help advance these [peace] efforts. Now is the time for Arab states to act on the initiative's promise by . . . taking steps toward normalizing relations with Israel."[86] In effect, while praising the initiative, Obama was reversing the order that the Saudis so valued. He was asking the Arabs to normalize relations as a goodwill gesture before Israel had made the massive concessions that the Arabs were demanding.

In June 2009, just prior to his massively touted speech to the Muslim world in Cairo, Obama arrived in Riyadh to try to wrest some Arab goodwill gestures. He expected the Saudis to play along, but was in for a rude awakening. He received a resounding rebuff from the Saudis, which included a reported tirade by King Abdallah. One Riyadh-based diplomat told the McClatchy Newspapers that it would be quite difficult for the Saudis to lead in the way the U.S. was proposing, because any warmth toward Israel would be deeply unpopular with the Saudi public.[87] This illustrated the strong connection between regional security and domestic security for the Saudis in the new strategic landscape.

The Saudis could not have been clearer. In their view, they had already made all the concessions necessary with their initiative. Both

Foreign Minister Saud al-Feisal and former Ambassador to the U.S. Turki al-Faisal tried to explain the Saudi position. Saud accused Israel of trying to shift the debate, when what it needed to do was end the occupation that began in 1967. He rejected the incremental approach pursued by the Obama administration. In an op-ed in the *New York Times*, Turki invoked Saudi Arabia's position as the birthplace of Islam, which, he argued, made Riyadh's recognition prized by Israel. Yet this was not in the cards, he maintained, unless Israel made a full withdrawal of all settlements.[88]

By early November, the Obama administration realized that its initial approach, based on a full settlement freeze in exchange for some minimal Saudi normalization steps, had failed; neither side was willing to go along, and the Arabs rejected an Israeli counter-proposal for a limited freeze.[89] In late November, the Israeli government announced a unilateral limited freeze. The Saudis remained unmoved.

SAUDI ARABIA is the most important Arab ally of the U.S., not least because of its vast oil supplies. Saudi Arabia's main concern is Iran and its influence on Saudi domestic stability, not the Arab-Israeli conflict. U.S. policymakers should be encouraged to cement the alliance with Saudi Arabia by resolutely addressing the Iranian threat to Saudi domestic politics and Riyadh's regional position. This U.S. policy would have the added benefit of reducing the Saudi desire to form security relationships with Russia and China. In 2008 Moscow and Riyadh signed a military cooperation agreement, and for a while there have been reports about a major arms deal with Russia, involving tanks, helicopters, and infantry-fighting vehicles to the tune of $2 billion. Recently another deal, involving the advanced S-400 missile-defense system, has been mooted.[90] This would not be the first time the Saudis had chosen to diversify their military suppliers. In the late 1980s, they made a secret purchase of nuclear-capable Chinese CSS-2 ballistic missiles, able to hit all countries in the region. It has been reported that Riyadh is now considering longer-range CSS-5 or CSS-6 missiles from China, or the Ghauri missile from Pakistan.[91] There is no doubt that these developments are due to the Iranian threat. A more robust U.S. response to Iran would reassure the Saudis and lessen their temptation to seek protection from U.S. rivals.

The kingdom also leads the six-member Gulf Cooperation Council. The assurance that the U.S. will clip Iran's wings will have a calming effect on the entire GCC, particularly Kuwait, Bahrain, and the U.A.E., which fear Iranian subversion. All the U.S. allies in the region need to know that they have strong, robust, and consistent U.S. backing to confront Iranian aggression. Then they will feel less of a need to call upon the services of America's strategic adversaries.

## NOTES

1. See Abdallah's interview with the Kuwait daily *Al-Siyasa*, January 27, 2007.

2. Joshua Teitelbaum (ed.), *Political Liberalization in the Persian Gulf* (New York: Columbia University Press, 2009).

3. See Joshua Teitelbaum, *The Rise and Fall of the Hashemite Kingdom of Arabia* (New York: New York University Press, 2001).

4. The other is the Hashemite Kingdom of Jordan, named after the Hashemite family.

5. Madawi Al-Rasheed, *A History of Saudi Arabia* (Cambridge: Cambridge University Press, 2002), p. 3.

6. For example, see Joshua Teitelbaum, "Pilgrimage Politics: The *Hajj* and the Saudi-Hashemite Rivalry," in Asher Susser and Aryeh Shmuelevitz, *The Hashemites and the Modern World* (London: Frank Cass, 1995), pp. 65–85. See also Joseph Kostiner, *The Making of Saudi Arabia, 1916–1936: From Chieftaincy to Monarchical State* (New York: Oxford University Press, 1993).

7. David Ottoway, "The U.S. and Saudi Arabia since the 1930s," presentation to the Foreign Policy Research Institute, June 25, 2009.

8. Ottoway, "The U.S. and Saudi Arabia since the 1930s."

9. Malcolm Kerr, *The Arab Cold War: Gamal 'Abd Al-Nasir and His Rivals, 1958–1970* (London: University Press, 3rd edn., 1971); Yezid Sayigh and Avi Shlaim

(eds.), *The Cold War and the Middle East* (Oxford: Clarendon Press, 1997); Galia Golan, *Soviet Policies in the Middle East: From World War II to Gorbachev* (Cambridge: Cambridge University Press, 1990).

10. For a critique of the Twin Pillars policy, see Howard Teicher, *From Twin Pillars to Desert Storm: America's Flawed Vision in the Middle East from Nixon to Bush* (New York: Willliam Morrow, 1993).

11. Jimmy Carter, State of the Union address, January 23, 1980.

12. Jimmy Carter, State of the Union address, January 23, 1980.

13. Ronald Reagan, *An American Life: The Autobiography* (New York: Simon and Schuster, 1990), p. 516.

14. Reagan, p. 523.

15. George Shultz, *Turmoil and Triumph: My Years as Secretary of State* (New York: Charles Scribner's Sons, 1993), p. 935.

16. Toby Jones, "Rebellion on the Saudi Periphery: Modernity, Marginalization and the Shi'a Uprising of 1979," *International Journal of Middle East Studies*, Vol. 38, No. 2 (May 2006), pp. 213–233. Fouad Ibrahim, *The Shi'is of Saudi Arabia* (London: Al Saqi, 2006).

17. Toby Jones, "Rebellion on the Saudi Periphery." While the regime was busy putting down a Shiite uprising in the Eastern Province, Wahhabi radicals took over the Great Mosque in Mecca. On this incident, see Teitelbaum, *Holier than Thou*, pp. 19–22, and Yaroslav Trofimov, *The Siege of Mecca: The Forgotten Uprising in*

*Islam's Holiest Shrine and the Birth of al-Qaeda* (New York: Doubleday, 2007).

18. Ibrahim, p. 33.

19. Hasan al-Saffar, *Kalimat al-Haraka al-Islamiyya*, p. 30, quoted in Ibrahim, p. 132.

20. Joshua Teitelbaum, *Holier than Thou*, pp. 98–113.

21. Thomas Heggehammer and Stéphane Lacroix, "Rejectionist Islam in Saudi Arabia: The Story of Juhayman al-Utaybi Revisited," *International Journal of Middle East Studies*, Vol. 39, No. 1 (January 2007), pp. 103–122. See also Yaroslav Trofimov, *The Siege of Mecca*.

22. See Martin Kramer, "Khomeini's Messengers in Mecca," in his *Arab Awakening and Islamic Revival* (New Brunswick: Transaction, 1996), pp. 161–87.

23. Teitelbaum, *Holier than Thou*, pp. 25–47.

24. Teitelbaum, *Holier than Thou*, pp. 73–82.

25. Teitelbaum, *Holier than Thou*, pp. 83–98.

26. FBI press release, June 21, 2001, and copy of indictment, http://www.fbi.gov/pressrel/pressrel01/khobar.htm.

27. ABC News, September 11, 2007, http://blogs.abc news.com/theblotter/2007/09/us-saudis-still.html.

28. Henry Schuster, "Poll of Saudis Shows Wide Support for bin Laden's Views," CNN, June 9, 2004, http://edition.cnn.com/2004/WORLD/meast/06/08/poll.binladen/index.html.

29. Ned Parker, "Conflict in Iraq: Saudi Role in Insurgency," *Los Angeles Times*, July 15, 2007.

30. Alexandra Zavis, "Foreign Fighters in Iraq Seek Recognition, U.S. Says," *Los Angeles Times*, March 17,

2008; "Saudis Biggest Group of al Qaeda Iraq Fighters: Study," Reuters, December 19, 2007; Tom Regan, "Report: Private Saudi citizens funding Iraqi insurgents," *Christian Science Monitor*, December 8, 2006; Richard Oppel, "Foreign Fighters in Iraq Are Tied to Allies of U.S. ," *New York Times*, November 22, 2007.

31. The latest series of arrests was in August 2009. See Robert Worth, "Saudi Arabia: Antiterror Arrests," *New York Times*, August 20, 2009. In mid-October, 2009, two Al-Qaeda terrorists disguised as women were killed in a clash near the Yemeni border. AP, October 14, 2009.

32. Mark McDonald, "Suicide Bomber Injures Saudi Prince," *New York Times*, August 29, 2009.

33. Jeffrey Fleishman, "Rehabbing Militants in Saudi Arabia," *Los Angeles Times*, December 21, 2007; Jason Burke, "Saudis Offer Pioneering Therapy for ex-Jihadists," *Guardian*, March 9, 2008; Christopher Boucek, "Extremist Reeducation and Rehabilitation in Saudi Arabia," Jamestown Foundation *Terrorism Monitor*, Vol. 5, No. 16, August 17, 2007; Brian Ross, "Trading Bombs for Crayons: Terrorists Get 'Art Therapy'," ABCNEWS, January 23, 2009.

34. The program has not been without its critics, and some prominent terrorists have returned to Al-Qaeda. See Robert Worth, "Two ex-Detainees in Qaeda Video," *New York Times*, January 25, 2009, and Robert Worth, "9 Alumni of Saudi Program for ex-Jihadists Arrested," *New York Times*, January 27, 2009. Still, to judge by the

drop in attacks, a combination of carrot and stick seems to be working.

35. AP, July 22, 2009.

36. Sudarsan Raghavan and Peter Finn, "U.S. Sees Saudi Plan as an Option for Detainees," *Washington Post*, October 14, 2009. This article describes how the Saudis combine tribal and family pressure with financial compensation. One former jihadist, Khalid al-Juhani, relates how his family and tribe keep constant watch over him and report his actions to the government. The government has provided him with a job, a car, and a well-furnished apartment.

37. Bernard Haykel, "Al-Qaida Stumbles in Saudi Arabia," *Guardian*, September 27, 2009.

38. Lars Berger, "Iran and the Arab World: A View from Riyadh," *Middle East Review of International Affairs*, Vol. 13, No. 3 (September 2009), pp. 24–33.

39. See, for example, *Al-Quds al-'Arabi*, October 17, 2009.

40. Joshua Teitelbaum, "Dueling for Da'wa: State vs. Society on the Saudi Internet," *Middle East Journal*, Vol. 56, No. 2 (Spring 2002), pp. 222–239.

41. BBC News, October 5, 2009.

42. On the lesser-known Venezuelan case, see Carlos Valdez, "Diplomat: Iran Opposes U.S. Base Deal for Colombia," AP, August 18, 2009.

43. On the Saudi-Iranian proxy war in Yemen, see Hakim al-Masmari, "Saudi-Iranian War Fought in Sa'ada," *Yemen Post*, August 31, 2009; Robert Haddick,

"The Middle East's Cold War Heats Up," August 28, 2009, www.foreignpolicy.com.

44. Jumana al-Tamimi, "Hezbollah Cell Worries Egypt," *Washington Times*, April 23, 2009.

45. Teitelbaum, "The Shiites of Saudi Arabia."

46. *Washington Post*, April 22; AFP, 23, 24 April; www.arabicnews.com, April 24; *Al-Quds al-'Arabi*, May 1; *Los Angeles Times*, May 8, 2003.

47. *Los Angeles Times*, April 26, 2006.

48. Demonstrations with participants carrying pictures of Hizballah leader Hasan Nasrallah were reported to have been held in Qatif in July and August. Several arrests were made. In October, during Ramadan, the authorities arrested four more Shiites after they brandished a Hizballah poster at a break-the-fast gathering. July 21, 2006, www.alrasid.net./artc.php?id = 12054; *Haaretz* (English edition), October 17, 2006.

49. AP, August 4, 5, 2006.

50. Federal Broadcast Information Service, OSC Report, August 16, 2006; *Middle East Times*, July 24, 2006.

51. See the article explaining Bin Jibrin's position on the Al-Arabiyya website at www.alarabiya.net/Articles/2006/08/08/26443.htm. See also Bin Jibrin's own explanation on his website at www.sona3el7yah.com/ftawa.php?view = vmasal&subid = 15294&parent = 4143.

52. Ibrahim, p. 197; Teitelbaum, *Holier than Thou*, p. 46.

53. www.islamlight.net/Files/Rwafeth/.

54. Federal Broadcast Information Service, OSC Report, August 16, 2006.

55. December 11, 2006, www.islamlight.net/index.php?option = content&task = view&id = 3818; Reuters, December 11, 2006.

56. December 17, 2006, albarrak.islamlight.net/index.php?option = com_ftawa&task = view&id = 18080&Itemid = 7, cited in Gause. See also FBIS, Saudi Clerics Roundup, February 19–23, 2007.

57. January 21, 2007, www.ibn-jebreen.com/printnew.php?page = 8.

58. October 24, 2006, www.middle-east-online.com.

59. *Kuwait Times*, November 21, 2006.

60. *Al-Siyasa*, January 27, 2007.

61. www.alfrqan.com/docs.phtp?docid = 65, February 28, 2007.

62. www.alrasid.com/artc.php?id = 9943, February 20, 2006.

63. FBIS OSC Report, May 11, 2007.

64. AP, January 30, 2007; *Los Angeles Times*, April 26, 2006; *New York Times*, February 5, 2007. Department of State, Saudi Arabia: Country Report on Human Rights Practices 2006, March 6, 2007.

65. FBIS OSC Report on terrorist websites, February 12, 2007.

66. AP, February 3, 2007.

67. *Christian Science Monitor*, January 18, 2007.

68. "Yemeni Shiite Cleric and Houthi Disciple Issam al-Imad: our Leader Houthi is Close to Khamenei; We

are Influenced Religiously and Ideologically by Iran," MEMRI, Special Dispatch No. 2637, November 2, 2009.

69. Intelligence and Terrorism Information Center, "Geopolitically Strategic Yemen Has Become a Focus of Local Iranian-Saudi Arabian Strife," October 1, 2009, http://www.terrorism-info.org.il/malam_multimedia/English/eng_en/html/iran_e025.htm; AP, August 18, 2009.

70. Yoel Guzansky, "Yemen's Increasing Importance in the Regional Struggle," *INSS Insight*, No. 128, September 9, 2009.

71. Reuters, October 19, 2009; PRESSTV, October 20, 2009.

72. Reuters, November 4, 2009.

73. Guzanksy, "Yemen's Increasing Importance."

74. Berger, "Iran and the Arab World."

75. Ewen MacAskill and Ian Traynor, "Saudis Consider Nuclear Bomb," *Guardian*, September 18, 2003, cited in Berger, "Iran and the Arab World"; Mark Lander and David Sanger, "Clinton Speaks of Shielding Mideast from Iran," *New York Times*, July 22, 2009; David Sanger, "Clinton Says Nuclear Aim of Iran is Fruitless," *New York Times*, July 26, 2009.

76. Quoted in Berger, "Iran and the Arab World."

77. Uzi Mahnaimi and Sarah Baxter, "Saudis Give Nod to Israeli Raid on Iran," *Sunday Times*, July 5, 2009.

78. Yossi Melman, "How Israel Managed to Hinder Iran Nuclear Plans," *Haaretz*, September 30, 2008.

79. In October, Iranian Foreign Minister Manouchehr Mottaki said that Iran had "evidence to suggest" that the U.S. was involved in Amiri's disappearance. AP, October 7, 2009.

80. Tariq al-Humayd, "It is Time to Uncover the Iranian Ploy," *Al-Sharq al-Awsat*, October 4, 2009.

81. "Saudi Dailies: Iran Encourages Terrorism, Sectarian Strife in Arab Countries," MEMRI, *Special Dispatch*, No. 2613, October 23, 2009.

82. Rachelle Kliger, "Saudi and Iran in pre-Hajj Tension," *Jerusalem Post*, October 28, 2009; Abd al-Rahman al-Rashid, "Iran's Battle at the Pilgrimage," *Al-Sharq al-Awsat*, November 2, 2009; BBCNEWS, November 3, 2009.

83. Roee Nahmias, "Wave of Arrests Follow Plot to Blow up Dubai Tower," *Yediot Aharonot*, September 15, 2009; Siham al-Najami, "Report about Iran Trying to Blow up Burj Dubai Not True, Top Official Says," *Gulf News*, September 15, 2009.

84. Joshua Teitelbaum, *The Arab Peace Initiative: A Primer and Future Prospects*, Jerusalem Center for Public Affairs, 2009.

85. AFP, March 28, 2002.

86. *Washington Post*, January 22, 2009.

87. Josh Rogin, "Revisiting Obama's Riyadh Meeting," *The Cable*, www.foreignpolicy.com, July 17, 2009; Dion Nissenbaum, "Despite Obama's Appeal, Saudis

Unlikely to Push Mideast Talks," *Miami Herald*, July 26, 2009.

88. Glenn Kessler, "No Incremental Steps for Peace, Saudi Says," *Washington Post*, August 1, 2009; Turki al-Faisal, "Land First, Then Peace," *New York Times*, September 13, 2009.

89. Karen DeYoung, "U.S. hope dims for high-level Israeli-Palestinian talks over state," *Washington Post*, November 4, 2009; Mark Lander, "Short-Term Fixes Sought in Mideast," *New York Times*, November 4, 2009.

90. See AFP, August 30, 2009, and AFP, October 1, 2009.

91. Berger, "Iran and the World"; Harsh Pant, "Saudi Arabia Woos China and India," *Middle East Quarterly*, Vol. 13, No. 4 (Fall 2006), pp. 45–52.

# ABOUT THE AUTHOR

JOSHUA TEITELBAUM is a senior fellow at Tel Aviv University's Dayan Center for Middle Eastern Studies and principal research associate at the Global Research in International Affairs Center, Interdisciplinary Center, Herzliya. He is currently a visiting fellow at the Hoover Institution and a visiting scholar at the Center on Democracy, Development, and the Rule of Law, both at Stanford University. A noted scholar on Saudi Arabia and the Persian Gulf, he is author of *Holier than Thou: Saudi Arabia's Islamic Opposition* and editor of *Political Liberalization in the Persian Gulf* (Columbia University Press, 2009).

Herbert and Jane Dwight
Working Group on
Islamism and the
International Order

HOOVER
INSTITUTION
STANFORD
UNIVERSITY

The Herbert and Jane Dwight Working Group
on Islamism and the International Order seeks
to engage in the task of reversing Islamic radicalism through reforming and strengthening
the legitimate role of the state across the entire
Muslim world. Efforts will draw on the intellectual resources of an array of scholars and practitioners from within the United States and
abroad, to foster the pursuit of modernity,
human flourishing, and the rule of law and reason in Islamic lands—developments that are

critical to the very order of the international system.

The Working Group is chaired by Hoover fellows Fouad Ajami and Charles Hill with an active participation of Director John Raisian. Current core membership includes Russell A. Berman, Abbas Milani, and Shelby Steele, with contributions from Zeyno Baran, Reul Marc Gerecht, Ziad Haider, R. John Hughes, Nibras Kazimi, Habib Malik, and Joshua Teitelbaum.

# INDEX